Life in Vietnam

The Essential Guide for Travellers

D1565203

DINGO
B O O K   C L U B

"Great Books Change Life"

Table of Contents

VIETNAM

Introduction

Vietnam is a country in Southeast Asia with a population of around 95 million, ranked 14 on the list of most populous countries. The country has a long beautiful coastline bordering the South China Sea. Vietnam is surrounded by:

- China in the north
- Laos in the northwest
- Cambodia to the southwest

Vietnam also has maritime borders with Thailand, Malaysia, Indonesia, and the Philippines. The country has a long history of influence with China. Replete with rich cultural history, quiet and contented lifestyle and great job opportunities, Vietnam is a melting pot of cultures with cultural and historical influences from China, France, India, Japan, and many other countries from the across the globe, in general, and from Asia, in particular.

Whether you want to visit Vietnam as a traveller or want to settle down there, this book will be immensely useful to know a lot about the country including:

- Its rich history dating back to the Palaeolithic age
- Its culture, language, and customs picked up from other cultures and given a Vietnamese twist
- The various religions practiced
- Lifestyle, housing, weather, and transportation
- Jobs, cost of living, and other pertinent details

Towards the end of the book, I have also added a small summary about the best and the worst in this beautifully amazing country. Despite a few issues, Vietnam is a bustling modern nation, which has opened up its economy to the world and offers its visitors a peek into its rich wonderful past while creating a suitable environment for new growth opportunities for everyone.

Backed by a society that believes in collectivism and overall goodness for everyone in the community, Vietnam is a great country to visit or even in which to settle down. Armed with the information given in this book, you will be able to manage the differences in cultures and lifestyle without much ado appreciating the beauty of your own culture and country while being open-minded about imbibing and learning about new countries and cultures.

After all, we are all human beings living on this planet, which is a mere speck of dust in this vast, expanding universe. So, go ahead and learn about Vietnam. The name, by the way, can be traced back to the second century BC to the then rulers of the country, the Trieu Dynasty. More about this, in the first chapter!

Chapter 1: History of Vietnam

Tomb of Khai Dinh Emperor, Hue

Most people commonly think of war when Vietnam comes to mind, thanks to the highly forgettable horrors of the Vietnam War. However, Vietnam's history is rich and beautiful filled with wonderful stories of valorous and great kings who left behind wonderful legacies for their country and its people.

The Beginning: Legends and History

According to Vietnamese folklore, Viet Nam was established when King Lac Long Quan, also referred to as the Dragon Lord of the Seas or the Dragon Lord of Lac, and Princess Au Co got married. Au Co was believed to be an immortal Chinese princess who came down from the high mountains to marry the Dragon Lord of the Seas. The legendary couple had 100 sons and their kingdom soon stretched from northern Indonesia to Southern China.

However, the loving couple was convinced that the vast differences between them because of coming from very different origins would never make them happy. So, they decided to separate from each other, each spouse getting 50 sons. Princess Au Co went back to her home in the High Mountains along with her set of 50 sons and King Lac Long Quan ruled over the lowlands with his set of 50 sons.

The king died in 2879 B.C., after which, Hung Vuong, his eldest son, established the Hung Dynasty in the lowlands. Hung Vuong is considered to be the founder of the first Vietnamese Dynasty, the Hung Dynasty, and the country of Vietnam. The name Viet Nam represents the formation of a new country by mingling of the northern High Mountains and the southern lowlands.

In fact, the French who combined it into one word, Vietnam, spelled Viet Nam as two words instead of one until the period of colonization. The concept of combining the northern mountains and the southern lowlands is repeated again and again throughout the history of the country.

The Hung Dynasty and Others That Followed

The Hung Dynasty was ruled by 18 kings. During their time, this region was called Van Lang. In 258 B.C, the Hung Dynasty was defeated by a neighboring king who founded a new kingdom called Au Lac and constructed a new capital at Phuc An. The remains and ruins of Phuc An can be seen even today at the Co Loa village, west of Vietnam's modern-day capital, Hanoi.

Nam Viet, King Trieu Da and the Fight for Freedom

About 50 years after the establishment of Au Lac kingdom, Trieu Da, a Chinese general, overthrew it and formed a nation named Nam Viet. Historians argue that until Trieu Da came into power, the legendary aspect of Vietnam finished. Trieu Da is considered to be the first true historical ruler of Vietnam. For about 100 years after Nam Viet was established, there was continued conflict between the Chinese Han emperors and King Trieu Da. In 111 B.C., Vietnam was completely annexed into the Chinese empire.

This was the beginning of the fight for freedom from the Chinese stronghold by the Vietnamese which went on for nearly 19 centuries after that first conquest. While the struggle for independence from Chinese power continued with short victories in between, until 939, the Chinese ruled, influenced, exploited and held their sway over Vietnam. In 939, the Tang Dynasty in China weakened considerably giving the resilient Vietnamese people the perfect opportunity to regain freedom, which they did under General Ngo Quyen. After this, Vietnam remained largely independent of foreign influence and a string of native 'Great Dynasties' ruled for the next 944 years.

Here is a brief timeline of the Great Dynasties of Vietnam:

939-967 – The Ngo Dynasty

Set up by General Ngo Quyen, this dynasty was caught in continued conflicts and battles with the Chinese despite gaining complete freedom.

968-980 – The Dinh Dynasty

Established by a feudal lord who was able to unify the entire country under his dominance

980-1009 – Early Le Dynasty

Buddhism became the dominant religion during this time. The northern part of Champa kingdom was annexed into Vietnam.

1009-1225 – The Ly Dynasty

The first emperor of this dynasty is believed to have had a dream in which he saw a dragon rise up from the ground and ascend into heaven. He moved the capital to the place in which the dream occurred which was in the city of Thang Long. This place was renamed as Hanoi later on. This is also the legend that is attached to the moniker of the Land of the Rising Dragon for Vietnam.

1225-1400 – The Tran Dynasty

This dynasty was responsible for fighting off Mongol attacks led by Kublai Khan. Marco Polo also traveled to Vietnam during the time of this dynasty; 1295.

1400-1428 – The Ho Dynasty

The point of note during the reign of the Ho Dynasty is, unfortunately, the victory of China again over Vietnam though it was only for a short while.

1428-1776 – The Later Le Dynasty

Under the able leadership of one of the kings of the Later Le Dynasty, King Le Loi, the invaders from China were fended off successfully and completely by the use of guerrilla tactics. The Late Le Dynasty is considered to be the Golden Period of Vietnam.

1543-1776 – The Trinh and Nguyen Rulers

Bitter civil wars broke the country into two halves in 1600 with the Trinh rulers controlling northern Vietnam and the Nguyen rulers controlling southern Vietnam leaving the Le Dynasty kings with little or no power though theoretically, they were still the ruling Dynasty.

During this time, the Nguyen rulers annexed the remaining part of Champa kingdom into Vietnam along with the Khmer empires in the east. These two annexations made Vietnam what it is today in terms of geographical area it covers.

1792-1883 – The Nguyen Dynasty

There were continued internal conflicts and revolts during this period. Yet, the country remained unified. The capital was moved to Hue and the current imperial splendor took place during this time of Vietnam history. The French missionaries who had landed in Vietnam by this time were proving to become very popular and prominent in their interactions with the Vietnamese rulers.

However, the rulers of the Nguyen Dynasty slowly became suspicious of the French missionaries, which turned to open hostility very soon. This hostile approach changed the course of Vietnam history in more ways than one.

The Colonial Expansion in Vietnam

French missionaries came to Vietnam in the 1700s and by the 19th century, they were a force to be reckoned with in Vietnamese politics. There was increasing suspicion and resentment that the Vietnamese felt against the French and soon the two sides clashed.

The French Invasion of Vietnam happened due to many reasons including:

- Expulsion and even killing of French missionaries
- France wanted to prove its dominion and military status as a colonial power to its European neighbors
- They wanted to capture strategic locations for improved international trade

- The Vietnamese people and rulers of that time were also in conflict about whether they should hold on to the older Confucianism or move on to becoming more modern and progressive

All the above factors drove the French ruler, Napoleon III, to give orders to his navy to attack the country in July 1857. Vietnam's military strength was no match for the sophisticated weaponry and modern military tactics of the French and they were forced to sign various treaties starting from 1862, which slowly but surely gave complete control of Vietnam to France in the following manner:

- Southern Vietnam fell to France in 1862 which they renamed as Cochinchina
- After 21 years in the year 1883, northern Vietnam was also captured by the French renaming it Tonkin
- Central Vietnam was renamed as Annam
- All three together became a French colony and was called Indochina

Colonization in Vietnam led to a lot of misery for the locals. Their natural resources were exploited, the people were treated badly and were extremely poor, and the Vietnamese leaders had absolutely no power to do anything. As expected, revolutions against the French started taking place and the most notable one was one that happened under the leadership of the Viet Nam Quoc Dan Dang Party.

Nguyen Tat Thanh, also called Nguyen Ai Quoc, a young revolutionary, took up arms against the French after training under the Chinese and the Russian communists. This man later became famous known as Ho Chi Minh. Along with him, many other groups also revolted against the French. Although these revolts happened sporadically, the Vietnamese people became more conscious about their desire for freedom and independence.

In World War II, when Japan was defeated, there was chaos and Ho Chi Minh took advantage of the situation and wrested a large part of the northern rural parts of Vietnam although the French continued to hold many of the cities in the region. After continued fighting and negotiations, the French finally agreed to cede power to the Vietnamese people in 1949, by putting up a puppet government under the toothless leadership of Bao Dai, a former Vietnamese Emperor. Ho Chi Minh refused to acknowledge the new leader and continued to urge the Vietnamese people and his soldiers to fight for their freedom.

Soon, the two teams on either side of multiple battles were clear. Ho Chi Minh with help from Russia and China fought against Bao Dai who had support from the US and the French. The French-supported Bao Dai was finally defeated in 1954. But all was not well yet for the Vietnamese people.

After France's defeat, the communists took over northern Vietnam, called the Democratic Republic of Vietnam, while the nationalists took over southern Vietnam, called the Republic of Viet Nam. As part of deliberations that took place after the war of 1954, it was also agreed to hold general elections across the entire country in the hope of unifying it.

17

However, southern Vietnam leaders, with help from their powerful ally, the US, never made the general election happen for fear of Ho Chi Minh coming out victorious. Instead of a peaceful general election process taking place, the Vietnamese people were witness to a bloody, devastating war that many of them are still trying to recover from.

The Vietnam/American War

While there would be little or no purpose in going into the morals and judgments about who was right and who was wrong in the war that shook Vietnam to its very core, the knowledge of what happened and the effects of that war are critical elements in the long history of the Vietnamese people to fight for their freedom.

After the 1954 defeat of the French, Vietnam was divided into two halves, the northern part held by Communists and the southern part by the people who represented modern-day democracy. During this time, the Vietnamese were given one year to choose to move to their side of the halved country.

Millions of people from northern Vietnam chose to move out from the clutches of the communists in the hope of living in a free democratically governed southern Vietnam. Most of the people who left northern Vietnam were forced to leave behind their property, homes and other possessions that were part of their families for generations. Contrarily, only about 10,000 people chose to move in the reverse direction; from southern Vietnam to northern Vietnam.

The unfortunate thing for the Vietnamese people was their lives were bad no matter which part of the country they chose to live in or move to. South Vietnam had oppressive governments right through that did little for the people of the country. Yet, these repressive governments continued to flourish in the south because of the support they had from their own military and that of the US.

In a bid to counter all these repressive governments, communists from the north and the south began to revolt and a lot of insurrection activities took place. These activities put the fear of communism in the minds of the US who believed that if communists won in Vietnam, there would be a domino effect and communism would spread to other countries as well resulting in undermining their military, political and economic power in a global scene. They were simply looking for a reason to directly attack Vietnam.

This unfortunate incident happened when communists from northern Vietnam supposedly attacked a US ship in 1964. The US President Lyndon at that time was President Johnson who passed the resolution of the Gulf of Tonkin. This resolution resulted in a full-scale US military attack on Vietnam. The number of US troops in Vietnam increased exponentially growing from 180,000 troops at the end of 1965 to 540,000 troops by the end of 1969.

The Vietnam/American War was launched with the superiority of the US military backed by their belief that the sophisticated weaponry would deflate the communists in no time. However, the Vietnamese people had perfected the guerrilla warfare over two millennia and soon, the US realized that they were on a losing path.

However, it was not so simple. The Vietnamese communists continued to attack US troops through guerrilla warfare and the politics between the US military and the US leaders back in their country resulted in a bloody war that left thousands and thousands of innocent Vietnamese civilians brutalized, raped or left for dead.

Soon, the bloody war began to be noticed by the world leaders and attracted the attention of the media as well and opposition to US involvement began to increase among the other nations of the world. The Vietnamese communists launched an offensive against the US on January 30, 1968, in which 36 cities in South Vietnam were attacked simultaneously. Yes, the communists' forces were defeated by the US army eventually.

However, the atrocities of that offensive and the counter effects swayed global public opinion and specifically US citizen opinion in favor of abandonment of the seemingly unending, expensive, unwinnable, and, perhaps, even immoral war in Vietnam. With mounting pressure from his own people and the leaders of the other nations of the world, President Richard Nixon, in 1972, began withdrawing US troops from southern Vietnam although he also ordered for the intensification of fighting in northern Vietnam.

In 1973, a final peace accord was signed which compelled the complete withdrawal of US troops from Vietnam. Well, the battles between the north and south of the country did not abate though there was no further intervention from the US.

The Cost of Brothers Fighting Amongst Themselves

By 1974, the US stopped sending aid to South Vietnam and it was clear to the people of this part of the country that they were facing imminent defeat. The North launched a full-scale offensive on its southern counterpart forcing the government in the south to surrender. This was, although appeared like a victory for the communists and defeat for the non-communists, was actually quite unfortunate for the people of Vietnam.

There were mass exoduses from southern Vietnam as people fled their homes and villages in fear of communist oppression and, perhaps, in fear of getting a payback from the northern Vietnamese. The war resulted in the deaths of nearly three-fourths of the Vietnam population. The land and economy were devastated and the lingering effects of that long and bloody war can still be felt. For the US, this war resulted in a huge dent in their self-confidence and the country is still fighting on the morals of what they did.

The result of war is always a tragedy for the common man irrespective of who wins or loses. And yet, the Vietnamese people have bounced back and, today, their community is thriving. People are keen on retaining their old-world charm replete with superstition, immense respect for elders, love for rice cultivation, and more amidst a booming economy that has brought alive the Vietnamese people as they try hard to leave behind the horrors of war and live a peaceful, happy, and contented life.

Today, tourism is a very active and productive industry, which is contributing to the booming economy of the country. People from all over the world are traveling to this quaint country and are amazed at the rich cultural heritage and the wonderful things they are discovering through their travels.

Chapter 2: Culture, Customs and Religion in Vietnam

The culture, customs and the ways of living in Vietnam might still appear as different and quite mysterious for people living outside the country. Today, as more people are traveling to this land for both personal and business reasons, the fascinating culture and customs of Vietnam are being revealed to the outside world. So, let's look at some of these customs of the Vietnamese people.

Superstitions in Vietnam

While belief in superstitions might baffle and befuddle the westerner, in Vietnam, it is a way of life. These traditions and customs have been passed on through generations. Yes, it is possible that some amount of ignorance, lack of scientific method and knowledge, and the acceptance of set traditions without question could play a big role in the continuation of superstitious beliefs in Vietnam even today. But, as outsiders, we must simply learn to respect and accept their beliefs.

Superstition plays a decisive role in many important aspects of a person's life including:

- How to keep a child healthy
- The charms embedded in a necklace have the power to keep out evil and keep the wearer safe
- Employees will not turn up for work on a particular day of a specific month because that day is unlucky.
- Someone will borrow money to purchase lottery tickets because he saw a fire in his dream the night before which is symbolic of winning money
- If you hear the hoot of an owl, it is considered a very bad omen and could bring illness and even death.
- Wars have been fought based on superstition in this country as they might choose not to attack on a particular day or time as the time does not bode well for the leader

In fact, superstition is so deeply embedded in the lives of the Vietnamese people that it is possible for a boy not to be able to marry the girl he loves because she was born in an inauspicious year.

The lunar calendar is followed by many Asian nations and there are some years, which are believed to be incompatible with other years. If people from incompatible times are married to each other, then misfortune and ill-luck will follow them throughout their lives! For example, a boy born in the Year of the Tiger should not marry a girl born in the Year of the Horse unless the couple is willing to risk exile and complete breaking away from their family ties.

There are many interesting stories about the practice of superstition in Vietnam. Here is an interesting one in Vietnam history that has become folklore: Nguyen Trai and Le Loi were generals who were leading an invasion against the Chinese. Nguyen Trai was a smart general and decided to leverage the power of superstition to his advantage. He got the following sentences written on leaves of all the trees in the forest: Le Loi for King, Nguyen Trai for Minister.

The ants ate up all the greasy parts leaving the message clearly embedded on the leaves. This 'prophecy' was noticed by all the people from the nearby villages and was seen as a message from the gods. They supported the war wholeheartedly and fought valiantly driving the Chinese out and putting Emperor Le Loi on the throne. There are many such stories about superstitions playing a very important role even in the modern day Vietnamese society.

Today, there are many social reformers who go around educating the people about the maladies of believing in superstitions without thought. Some young people of the country are also fighting a social war to outlaw the practice of superstition in Vietnam.

Village Guilds in Vietnam

Vietnam is primarily a rural state with many people engaged in the wet cultivation of rice. Since the beginning of the nation, native villages and lands have played an important role in the lives of the Vietnamese.

People gathered together and formed village associations and guilds, which developed and matured slowly but surely. With each passing generation, these guilds became stronger and more intertwined with the people with each village guild having its own set of rules, regulations and conventions that people of that particular village were bound to follow.

The purpose of the conventions of each of these village guilds was to keep alive the traditions and customs of that particular people. While the guilds are very different from each other, state laws bind them all in modern times. Many remnants of these guilds from earlier times are kept in various museums in the country for visitors to see and enjoy.

Ancestor Worship in Vietnam

Huyen Khong Cave with shrines, Marble mountains, Da Nang

Ancient worship was introduced to the Vietnamese people by the Chinese who captured and ruled over this land for nearly over 100o years from as far back as 2 B.C. Combined with the spread of Confucianism, ancestor worship forms an intrinsic part of the society fundamental social and religious practice. Ancestor worship binds the people of Vietnam together in a powerfully strong social and religious grip. The custom of ancestor worship is one of the most difficult things to understand by the westerners who travel to this land.

Every house, every office and every business place will have an altar commemorating the ancestors. Incense sticks are burned at the altar and as a token of respect fruits, gifts and sweets are offered. Paper replicas of money, cars, houses, bikes and more are offered too. After the offering, these paper replicas are burned so that the spirits of the offered gifts will rise up to the heavens for the ancestors to use.

Fruits are offered at the ancestor altar, Vietnam

In the earlier times, a part of the income earned from tilling the land was kept aside for the purpose of ancestor worship. This practice is not followed in the present day. However, the eldest son is expected to arrange and prepare the ceremonial requirements of ancestor worship after the death of his parents.

Ancestor worshipping rituals are conducted on specific days such as the new moon, the full moon and festival days. These rituals are also observed on the death of a family member. Also, these ancestor worship rituals are carried out on important events such as housewarming ceremonies, the birth of a child, starting off a new business or whenever someone in the family needs spiritual guidance.

Vietnamese home altar

Ancestor worship among the Vietnamese people is not based on any 'ghostly' or even spiritual intentions. They believe that their ancestors are still living in a different realm and it is the duty of the living to ensure their comfort in that realm. The ancestors, in return for this comfort, give advice and guidance to their children and grandchildren who are living in the earthly realms.

There are some ancestors who find a place in the temples of Vietnam. For example, the Trung sisters who lost their lives while fighting valiantly against the Chinese more than two millennia ago are now gods in almost every temple of Vietnam. Another heroic ancestors who has a place in temples is Tran Hung Do. These people's heroism and brave attitude are meant to guide the living.

Yes, there are 'bad' ancestors as well whose bad behavior is bound to bring ill-luck and misfortune to their children and future generations. This is used to instill a discipline of good behavior in the living so that their future generations are always showered with good luck and good fortune.

Ancestor worship is an important element in the culture and customs of Vietnam.

Funeral Customs of Vietnam

Solemn organization of funeral rites is an imperative part of the Vietnamese culture. While it has been simplified from the earlier elaborate rituals and rites, even in the modern times, the family members cover and place the body in a coffin. There is a funeral procession followed by the burial and regular visits to the tomb thereafter. The family members of the dead person wear a black band or a white turban as a symbol of mourning.

There are some old families who still follow the older and more elaborate customs, which include:

- The body is bathed and dressed
- The family members put a chopstick between the teeth of the deceased.
- They then place a tiny bit of rice along with the three coins in the mouth
- Now, the body, wrapped in a white-cloth covered grass mat, is placed in the coffin
- After the burial, which is accompanied with rituals, the family members observe three days of mourning
- The family members then visit the burial place and open the tomb again for worship and bring rice everyday to the altar
- The 100th day is celebrated as the 'end of tears' or 'tot khoc' followed by a ceremony for the first year anniversary
- The end of the second year is mourning festival

Vietnam Customs for Longevity

Even today, there are associations for longevity for the old in the villages of Vietnam. As longevity has improved for human beings, Vietnamese traditions have always moved up the 'old age' barrier. In the earlier days, when a man or woman reached 40 years of age, he or she was honored as an old person.

In the 12th and 13th centuries during the reign of the Tran dynasty, an emperor who reached the age of 40 gave up his throne to his succeeding heir and joined the Buddhist monastery as a monk. In the villages, after a man reached 50, he could no longer hold any official position in the village guild. While during festivals and other important events, they were invited, given a seat of honor on red-bordered mats, and were treated with a lot of respect.

Even today, the elderly are highly respected by the young. As a mark of love and respect for their parents and grandparents, children celebrate longevity festivals at 60, 70, and 80 years of age. These longevity ceremonies are usually held on their birthdays. In modern times, when women reach the age of 70 or 80, they are given gifts including red dresses.

Religions and Important Places of Worship in Vietnam

Today, the Vietnamese government is communist and, therefore, is an atheist entity. Yet, all religions are respected and allowed to be followed privately by the citizens of the country. While many modern Vietnamese categorize themselves as non-religious, they are not atheists by nature and follow religious practice and behaviours in their private lives. They visit temples and monasteries on important festival days every year.

The majority religion in Vietnam combines the tenets of three religions including Confucianism, Daoism and Buddhism. The combination of these three is called as Tam Giao in Vietnam and the customs and rituals are picked up from all three. A large percentage of Vietnamese regularly visit Buddhist pagodas. However, they are not pure Buddhists. They follow a syncretic combination of the three religions mentioned above. Today, Tam Giao, or the Triple Religion pervades every aspect of Vietnam life and culture.

Confucianism

Established in China between 5th and 6th century B. C, Confucianism came to Vietnam as far back as 1 A.D. when Chinese power began its domination on the region. Confucianism is less of a religion and more of a system that contains codes of behavior designed for the well-being and improvement of any given society. There is little talk of God and spirituality and more about how people should conduct themselves socially and in family settings.

The five important virtues that Confucianism exhorts its followers to imbibe are:

- Benevolence
- Righteousness
- Propriety
- Wisdom
- Fidelity

Confucianism created moral codes based on five important relationships in society including:

- Subject and ruler
- Husband and wife
- Children and parents
- Sisters and brothers
- Friends and friends

Although Confucianism declined with the advent of the French missionaries, the values of this religion influence the behavior and thinking of the Vietnamese people even today.

Daoism

Dao means road or way in the Chinese language. Daoism, like Confucianism, started in China as a philosophy rather than as a religion. Founded by Laozi in the 6th century B.C., it is believed that Confucius and Laozi met with each other and the former spoke highly of the latter.

Confucius focused on man and his behavior in society whereas Laozi focused on creating a harmonious connection between man and nature. To achieve this harmony, Daoism preaches a life free from conflicts and confrontations and imbibing good morals such as patience, simplicity and contentment.

After Laozi's passing away, many of his followers converted his philosophy into a dogmatic religion replete with priests, clergymen and temples. When the Tran Dynasty ended around the middle of the 15th century, Daoism turned to polytheism and mysticism. Now, this religion allows communication and prayers to spirits, a variety of deities and the dead too. Veneration of the spirit of ancestors, explained earlier, is widely practiced by the Vietnamese.

Buddhism

Buddhism came to Vietnam in 2 B.C. It was adopted as the state religion during the reign of the Later Le Dynasty that ruled Vietnam between 1010 and 1214. Even though after this period, Buddhism lost its position as a state religion the majority of the Vietnam people believed in its teachings and followed it.

Today, many Vietnamese identify themselves as Buddhists. However, they do not actively participate in many rituals that are conducted in Buddhist pagodas. Most of Vietnam follows the Mahayana Buddhism, which is also practiced in its neighboring countries such as Cambodia, Myanmar and Laos. However, in the Mekong Delta region, the Theravada sect of Buddhism is largely followed.

There is an amazing fact to give you an idea of how deeply the three religions of Confucianism, Daoism, and Buddhism were revered by the people of Vietnam. During the 11th and 12th century, recruitment to government jobs required applicants to write essays on the 'three religions.'

Other than the above three major religions practiced in Vietnam, there are some minority yet prominent religions as well including Christianity (Catholicism and Protestantism) and new religions like Hao and Cao Dai.

Cao Dai and Hao

These were new religions established around the beginning of the 20th century in southern Vietnam. Cao Dai combines tenets and values from Buddhism, Christianity, Confucianism, and even from people like Victor Hugo. Followers of Cao Dai follow practices from all these religions and include prayers, veneration of ancestors, vegetarianism, and non-violence. Hao is considered to be a sub-sect of Theravada Buddhism.

Christianity

Notre Dame Cathedral, Sai Gon

Catholicism is the most widespread branch of Christianity practiced in Vietnam. Introduced by the Portuguese and French missionaries in the 16th century, Catholicism in Vietnam received a huge boost during French rule. Canadian missionaries introduced the Protestant faith into Vietnam in the beginning of the 20th century.

Famous Temples & Places of Worship

The Thien Mu Pagoda

Thien Mu Pagoda (Pagoda of the Celestial Lady), Hue

Is located in central Vietnam in the city of Hue and is popularly referred to as the Pagoda of Celestial Lady. It was constructed in 1601 under the auspices of the first Nguyen. During the Vietnam War, this pagoda became a hotspot for anti-government activities when Catholicism was given preferential treatment over Buddhism. Again, in the 1980s, this pagoda was the hub of anti-Communist activities.

The Thien Hau Temple and Fujian Assembly Hall

Thien Hau Temple, Sai Gon

This temple is dedicated to Mazu, the Fujian sea goddess who was also called Thien Hau. Referred to as the Pagoda of Lady Thien Hau, this temple was constructed by the Cantonese community in Sai Gon.

Originally built to serve the purpose of an assembly hall, the Fujian Assembly Hall in Hoi An became a place of worship again dedicated to Thien Hau. It is a popular place of worship for childless couples that leave offerings of fresh fruits with prayers for a child.

Other Facets of Vietnamese Culture

Languages Used

Vietnamese is the official language of the country and is somewhat similar (at least in its tonal quality) to Khmer, the language of Cambodia. Vietnamese is not an easy language to pick up as each syllable can be used in six different tones and each tone has a different meaning and definition.

Other languages spoken in Vietnam include Khmer, Cham, Chinese and some that are unique to the mountainous tribes of the country. In its written form, Vietnam uses Roman alphabets and accent marks to reflect the tone of use. This writing system is called quoc ngo and was set up in the 17th century by Catholic missionaries when they translated the scriptures to Vietnamese. Before this system came into place, another form called chu nom with Chinese characters was used for writing. However, since WWI, the quoc ngo system is used extensively across the country.

The Family in Vietnamese Culture

Consisting of both extended and nuclear types, the Vietnamese life and culture revolves around families. It is fairly common to see families where three generations of people are living together under the same roof. They follow Confucianism tenets of family life wherein the father is the head and it is his duty to provide for his family. The father is the person to take important decisions too. This same tradition moves into the spirit worship of ancestors and they are revered through worship during important festivals and on the birth or death of someone in the family.

Face

This is a little difficult concept for westerners to understand. Here is a simple explanation of the importance of 'face' in Vietnamese culture. It reflects an individual's prestige, dignity and standing in society. For example, it is possible to give face, to lose face, to save face, etc. What does each mean?

Losing face translates to being insulted or humiliated in public. A foreigner has to take care of his or her choice of words when they are talking to a Vietnamese because inadvertently someone could end up 'losing face' because of what is said. Complimenting and showing gratitude are examples of 'giving face' to someone.

Collectivism and Hierarchy

The Vietnamese culture is founded on collectivism which means that an individual's needs and desires come after those of the society of community they belong to whether it is the family, society or the country. Driven by this sense of collectivism, there are guidelines expected to be followed by everyone concerned with regard to protecting the group or community face.

Like any other well-organized and well-structured group or community, there is a strict hierarchical structure with all aspects of Vietnamese culture and business. The hierarchical structure is based on status and age. Again, this culture is an offshoot of Confucianism values, which focuses on social order.

Every person in a group or business or family has a specific place and a role. A classic example is evident in social gathering where the eldest in the group is always served and/or greeted first. Within a family, the head is responsible for taking important family decisions such as approving marriages.

Vietnamese Social Etiquette

There is a good amount of social etiquette that is expected to be followed in Vietnamese society. It is important to know and follow them well:

- Physical displays of affection in public with people of the opposite sex is not an accepted norm
- Touching someone's head or shoulder is not allowed. Neither should you pass anything over anyone's head
- When you pass items to other people, always use both hands
- Use your hand, and not your finger, to point out
- Standing with your hands on your hips or with your arms crossed over your chest is not allowed

- Shorts are allowed to be worn - only on a beach though. In modern cities, this can be waived. If you are invited for a party, please ask your host about dress code before taking a decision on what to wear. Dressing conservatively and modestly is usually expected in Vietnam

Vietnamese Business Etiquette

One of the most effective ways of doing business in Vietnam is to go through a local who will also act your interpreter or translator. Punctuality is important in this country and it is expected of everyone. Dressing conservatively can endear you to your Vietnamese business partners. When you present your business card, always do so with both your hands.

In business too, hierarchy plays an important role. During a meeting, the senior most person will usually enter the room first. Disagreements are usually shown with silence with the intention of 'saving face' for the other person. Most of the time, initial meetings are only for 'getting-to-know.' Negotiations and red tape can mean it takes a bit of time to set up your business. Therefore, you must come mentally and physically prepared for this.

Giving of Gifts

If you are invited for dinner to a Vietnamese house always carry a colorfully wrapped gift. Ensure the gift is not anything in black. Also, avoid yellow flowers. Chrysanthemums are associated only with funerals and, therefore, cannot be taken as gifts when you go visiting. Gift-giving in Vietnam is viewed differently from how a westerner views it. Based on Buddhist philosophy, giving gifts is more beneficial to the giver than to the receiver as acts of generosity increases good karma in the life of the giver.

It is a common thing to see that your host does not open the gift you brought for him. It is important to understand that this is not an act of insult or that he is not grateful. It is just that he prefers opening it later on. Common gifts that are exchanged include fruit, flowers (except chrysanthemum), chocolates, alcohol, etc.

Dining Etiquette and Table Manners

Here are some basic table manners that all Vietnamese follow diligently:

- The eldest member of the family always sits first
- Wait to be guided to your seat
- Pass dishes using both hands
- A flat spoon and chopsticks are used for eating
- Chopsticks have to be placed on the table after taking a few mouthfuls as well as when you are taking a break from eating to drink or to talk. When you finish eating, then the chopsticks have to be placed on the rice bowl.
- Ensure you finish everything on your plate

So, you see, Vietnam combines the old-world charm and yet manages to have a booming economy. It is, therefore, important to know, understand and respect the culture and customs of this ancient nation.

Chapter 3: Lifestyle in Vietnam

Two kinds of smells pervade Vietnam, no matter where you go; the smell of fish sauce (nuoc-mam) and the smell of burning incense. If you ask a Vietnamese about these two, he will say that the former represents the materialistic aspect of life and the latter represents the spiritual aspect of life. Wherever you go, whether it is to someone's home or to the numerous temples or the spirit houses, the smell of incense sticks will follow you.

The Vietnamese were, and still are, quite good at converting seemingly waste products into something useful. The fact that it is not a very rich country and many live below the poverty line gives you an indication of their need for thrift in their lives. For example, in the olden days, coconut shells were made into ladles or even used as containers. Today, a lot of modern brands have seen success in the country ranging from toilet paper to pens. Cheap champagne made in Vietnam is also available.

From taking baths in flooding rice fields to five siblings sharing one room, the people of Vietnam have found the boom in the economy a very liberating thing. Today, the market is flooded with television sets, mobile phones and other electronic devices. The young people of rural Vietnam have taken advantage of job opportunities in the urban areas and have moved up in life with access to a lot of modern amenities including staying in larger accommodations, access to washing machines, etc.

Possessions and Lifestyle in Rural Vietnam

If you have to walk into an average village home in rural Vietnam, you are very likely to see the following things:

- A couple of chairs and some tables
- Frame beds
- A television
- A small altar
- Portraits of family members and some houses keep a photo of Ho Chi Minh

Mattresses are a luxury item in the villages and most sleep on thin mats spread out on the hard floor. The houses are quite small and the food is cooked on crude handmade stoves that use charcoal for fuel.

The walls of the front rooms, ancestral shrines and altars are usually lined with photos of deceased loved ones. All members will light incense sticks in front of these pictures and pray to them. During the New Year festival, Tet, these altars are decorated with flowers, fruit and incense. A few houses have Buddhist altars set up outside the house in the front yard.

Another common superstitious belief is that after Tet, family members hang chicken feet near the front of their houses to keep evil spirits out of their homes and lives. If these feet turn black, then the family believes that the following year will bring them bad luck.

Another not-so-western thing about Vietnam is anger management is not taught, but rather, deeply imbibed in them.

Showing your anger is a sign of weakness and results in face loss of the targeted person. You are expected to know how to manage your anger and keep your temper in check. Westerners have a lot of learn from the calm and patient Vietnamese.

Possessions and Lifestyle in Urban Vietnam

The major cities in Vietnam include Ho Chi Minh City, Hanoi (which is the capital of Vietnam), Haiphong, Hue, and Da Nang. The cities of Vietnam cannot be compared with those of developed countries. Here too, the apartments are quite cramped. Until recently, electricity was also not fully available in cities either. People cooked outside their homes on stoves made with bricks.

In the absence of electricity, trees were painted white so that they could be seen during the nights. Fresh and perishable fruits and vegetables are usually brought in to the cities at midnight when the temperatures are lowest. Urban cities are flooded with people between planting and harvest seasons when farmers and agriculturists do not have work and need to earn a living. The government is making efforts to convert the economy into a cashless one and encouraging people to open bank accounts. The government is working on changing all this for the better.

Markets in Vietnam

Markets are not just a place to buy things but also one where people socialize, exchange cooking tips and bring fresh groceries daily. Unlike the western concept of cooking once a week and refrigerating it, the Vietnamese people believe in cooking fresh food every day. It is a common belief among Vietnamese that living near is a market and living near a river are the two most wonderful things in the life of a human being.

There are three types of markets in Vietnam including:

- Countryside Markets
- Highland Markets
- Floating Markets

Countryside Markets

Many villages in Vietnam host cho que or countryside markets. There are two types of countryside market; the evening market and the fair. While fairs are held periodically depending on the local custom of the particular village in question, evening markets are held every day where villagers can buy local, fresh produce for their daily meals. The large fairs attract visitors from outside the commune as well.

Local market in Hoi An

Highland Markets

Also referred to as Cho Tinh (Love Markets), these highland markets are set up in places where minorities live. In addition to being a commercial attraction, these highland markets are also places where the culture and customs of the minorities can be seen. People come dressed in their best clothes and spend a lot of time at these markets. They sing, dance, play the pan-flute and make new friends. That is the reason why the name Love Market is given to these events.

Highland market of H'mong people, Bac Ha, Vietnam

Floating Markets

Floating market in Can Tho, Vietnam

These floating markets are found in the Mekong River Delta. Known as cho noi these floating markets consist of thousands of boats filled with goods and produce. This market of hectic economic activity lasts right through the day, although the best time to go is in the morning when you can buy the freshest produce that the boats will offer. The largest floating markets in Vietnam are:

- Phong Dien Phung Hiep, and Nga Bay in Hau Giang
- Cai Rang in Can Tho
- Cai Be in Tien Giang

Floating market in Tien Giang, Vietnam

A large part of the agricultural produce sold in these floating markets is picked up by wholesalers who then resell them to processing factories and other retail markets.

Floating market in Hau Giang, Vietnam

Bargaining is a Way of Life in Vietnam

Vietnamese barter and bargain over the prices of everything ranging from vegetables to hair bands. Yet, it is important to note that bargaining takes place in a very polite environment as you already know that the Vietnamese people are averse to a show of anger and rudeness and expect the same of everybody.

The purpose of bargaining is not to get as close to the market price of the commodity as possible. Instead, the purpose is to make sure both sides of the bargain walk away thinking that it has achieved the best deal possible for everyone. Both parties walk away with the satisfaction they have not only not been cheated but have also made a killing. Bargaining is not about commerce and negotiations. It is about socializing too.

Here is a classic example of a bargaining tactic gone wrong for a westerner, who does not get the true purpose of negotiation. Suppose you are a westerner and you find this amazing piece of embroidered work and you ask to buy it at the price of $10 (of course, in the local Vietnamese currency which is Vietnamese Dong). The locals quote $15. You, being the typical Westerner who believes that time is money, simply offers to split down the middle and say you are ready to give $12.5 thinking you are smart and they will be happy with the extra $2.5!

However, the locals will withdraw and get into a huddle and talk among themselves stating that if this person is willing to up the price so easily, then their initial quote was too little. So, they come back with a new quote of $20! They haggle for some time and as a westerner, you are ambivalent thinking it would not be right to back down because you started the offer and yet, you are tired and time is after all money for you.

At this juncture, you remember that their original price was $15 and you make the suicidal move of buying the item at that original price. Now, perspectives have changed again for the locals and they realize that it was a mistaken upper limit earlier. The quote now goes up to $25. So, you see the logic of bargaining lies in the effect of getting the best deal not the actual cost of the product.

Food and Diet

Vietnamese diets are essentially very balanced and healthy. A typical Vietnamese meal consists of rice, fish and vegetables. Cooking methods used are stir-frying and/or steaming. Rice is the staple consumed three times a day with a side of meat/fish and vegetables. Pho or breakfast soup made with chicken or beef broth is another common dish all over Vietnam.

Nuoc mam or fish sauce is the most common ingredient in Vietnam cooking. The lack of milk and dairy products results in a shortage of calcium in the diet. In fact, many Vietnamese are lactose-intolerant too. Vietnamese diets are high in sodium (because of the excessive use of fish sauce) and low in fibers (because of a lack of whole grains).

Fasting is a common method of overcoming sickness. The Vietnamese believe that drinking hot water when you are sick with a little bit of thin rice gruel is best to give your digestive system some rest to recuperate and get your illness out of your body. The Vietnamese believe in combining hot and cold foods (balancing the yin and yang) to stay healthy. Therefore, they eat mangoes, garlic and beef (hot foods) and balance it by eating greens, pork and melons (cold foods).

There is a strange ambivalence regarding dogs among the Vietnamese. Dog meat is considered a delicacy (in fact, superstitious beliefs are rampant that dog meat enhances libido for men) and dogs are also seen as man's best friend! The ambivalence is more because of the difference in the generation gap. While the older men look at dog meat as a delicacy, the younger ones are finding it more and more difficult to kill the four-legged loyal friend for their meat.

Entertainment, Health and Fitness

Watching television and singing karaoke are the two most popular forms of recreation and entertainment in Vietnam. Modern Vietnamese youth like to hang out at cafes while chatting with their friends. Many men can be found in bai om or the karaoke bar with private hostesses and private rooms or in bia hoi, the common street side bar which serves beer made fresh daily.

The Vietnamese people are very health conscious and use a combination of the ancient and modern forms of exercises to keep fit and eat healthy. As an expatriate, there are lots of gyms ranging from the low-cost to the premium ones that dot nearly all the cities in this country where you will find local also sweating it out.

The Vietnamese version of tai chi is a common form of exercise to keep fit. You can find people engaged in tai chi postures and movements in public parks individually, which is quite unlike the Chinese version in which tai chi is performed as a group exercise. Modern entertainment options such as bowling and playing golf have also become fashionable among the wealthier set of Vietnamese population.

Rice Culture in Vietnam

Rice is an intrinsic part of the Vietnamese life. More than 75% of the population of Vietnam lives in villages engaged in farm and agricultural work. They earn their income by growing and cultivating rice. In Southeast Asia, the cultivation of rice can be dated to nearly 7,000 years ago. In Vietnam, rice is not just food; it is a symbol of culture. It is made as offerings at every ceremony and festival.

Lowland rice, also referred to as wet rice, is the most common type of rice grown and consumed in Southeast Asia including Vietnam. Some aspects of rice cultivation have become mechanized though a large number of small farmers still use manual labor to plant, reap, and thresh grain. Rice dryers are used all over the country to dry the rice after which they are milled.

Every part of the rice processing gives some kind of by-product none of which is wasted. Rice products are used to make puddings, noodles, cosmetics, wine and even cooking oil. The rice kernels are, of course, eaten and the rice stalks are converted to straws, which are then used to make hats, sandals, brooms, ropes, and thatched roofs as well.

Farmers are planting rice in Vietnam

The bumper rice crop in Vietnam happened in 1989, when there was record paddy output of 18.9 million tons. From a country that witnessed acute food shortage, Vietnam has turned around greatly and today, it is the second largest producer of rice to export in the world. And this is after making sure the domestic demands are met in full.

Rice Terraces in Sapa, Vietnam

After the debilitating Vietnam War, it is heartening to see rural life on its path to recovery, thanks to the increasing popularity of Vietnamese rice as its fragrance waft through millions of kitchens all over the globe.

Chapter 4: Housing in Vietnam

Vietnam is fast becoming the country of choice for many expats to either work in or even choose to retire to. With a quality of life that is better in many ways compared to other neighboring countries and at a fraction of the cost, more and more expats are choosing Vietnam as their home. Of course, the diverse and delicious food is another great motivation for most expats.

Here is how expats are more or less distributed in Vietnam:

- There is a big entrepreneurial group of expats living in Ho Chi Minh City along with a large chunk of technologists
- There are expats who work as teachers in Hanoi (I have another chapter that focuses only on job opportunities for expats)

- Many Vietnam War American soldiers have chosen to make Vietnam their home and can be found scattered all over the country

Like in most countries, living expenses can vary depending on a person's lifestyle. Yet, it is possible for any expat to live a fairly good life without burning a hole in his or her pocket. The biggest amount of the monthly budget would be towards housing, schools, and, perhaps, to buy things that are imported from the west. Phone, internet, and travel costs are relatively low.

Being part of Asia, Vietnam has a huge spread of electronic gadgets to tempt you. It is possible to buy these gadgets impulsively giving in to your deep electronic geek desires (a common thing among many Westerners). Yet, with a bit of care and financial shrewdness, it is possible to live well on an expat's salary in Vietnam and save money too.

Let's get down to housing in Vietnam. Most expats who come to this country to work or with an intention of checking it out before deciding to make it their home, find it easier and simpler to rent out homes instead of outright purchasing them. Like in most countries, house rental prices are dependent on the type of housing and the location.

There are multiple modern housing complexes and apartments that are coming up in all the important cities of Vietnam. Therefore, expats have a wide variety of luxury accommodations and not-so-luxury accommodations to choose from. Most of these apartment complexes come with many modern amenities including swimming pools, well-equipped gyms, laundries and more. Yes, the cost of these apartments will be higher than those without the availability of the amenities. Generally speaking, homes closer to the city center are more expensive than those farther away.

Types of Houses in Vietnam

One-Floor Houses

While single-floor houses have the luxury of creating a harmonious family atmosphere, it does need a lot of land to build one that can house all the required things for the convenience of all at home. Moreover, land does not come cheap or easy in bustling and growing cities. Therefore, in urban areas, single-floor houses account for only 20-30%. For the same reasons, single-floor homes in rural areas account for nearly 80-90% of the total accommodations.

Rural Homes

These homes serve the purposes of farmers living in the villages of Vietnam. Quaint and beautiful 1-2 storied homes serve both residential and agricultural production purposes of farmers. These kinds of homes usually have space to manage the harvest of wet rice. Moreover, rural homes are usually equipped with cages and other kinds of animal homes spread all over the courtyard.

City Villa

Definitely a high-end luxury accommodation type, city villas are usually for the ultra-rich locals and expats. They are surrounded by beautifully tended gardens and, normally located in the outskirts of a city (but within easy reach too). This type of home comes with large swimming pools and all the other modern amenities needed for a luxurious lifestyle.

Adjacent Block Homes

Here, each family will have a private plot of its own and yet, these plots are so close to each other that only the front and/or backspace will be available for gardening or any other options. Unlike the villas, there is not much of space all around in the adjacent block homes type of housing.

Apartment Complexes

Like in many other places, there are apartment complexes with self-contained living spaces for each family with shared amenities including corridors and staircases.

Housing Rentals

The monthly rent for a furnished apartment of about 900 square feet located in an expensive area (closer to the city center) would be about $850 and moves upwards depending on the amenities available, the size, and other factors. On the same lines, a furnished apartment of 900 square feet in a less expensive locality would be in the range of $500-$550.

Studio apartments in expensive areas will cost about $500 per month while in a less expensive area, the monthly rent would be $300. The electricity, heating and other utility costs will be apart from the amounts mentioned.

Ease of Finding Homes for Rent

Finding a home to rent and live in is a very easy process in Vietnam. While rental sites are good, you will not need them so much in Vietnam. After you have done your survey and chosen which locality of the city you want to live in, you can simply choose to walk around the area and you will find plenty of buildings, houses, apartments and rooms for rent. You can also find the highly westernized condominiums in the bigger cities of the country.

There are affordable real estate agents available at each locality/district that can help you find suitable accommodations as well. These agents also help you negotiate rents and the minimal fee usually is billed to the renter.

Buying Your Home in Vietnam

Foreigners or locals cannot own land. All land belongs to the state. As it is a communist state, all land is theoretically collectively owned by the citizens of the country and, of course, regulated by the state. Foreigners can buy a house or the dwelling place. However, they cannot own the land on which the house is built. They can only lease the land from the state. Buying property is only a transfer of leasing rights.

Today, there are options for 50-year leases, which are like a sale anyway. These leases give you a right over an apartment for 50 years renewable at the end of the term if you wish. Of course, there are other clauses as well to these lease agreements. Moreover, foreigners cannot sublease these dwelling houses. If they leave the country before the end of the lease, then the state takes over the property and the house certificates will cease to be valid.

Chapter 5: Transport, Visa and the Weather in Vietnam

There are various ways you can travel in and around Vietnam ranging from the simple 'cyclos' to a motorbike taxi to flying around in planes. All kinds of transportation options are available to you. Again, the options you choose are dependent on many factors including time availability, flexibility, budget and your sense of adventure.

Traveling

a) Flying in Vietnam

With over 20 airports servicing the country - many of which have been converted from landing strips that were built during the Vietnam War - you have a lot of choices in terms of flying. Most of the international flights land at Ho Chi Minh City in Saigon and in Hanoi. There are daily arrivals from many Asian cities including Seoul, Bangkok, Singapore, Hong Kong, Siem Reap (Cambodia), Guangzhou and Phnom Penh.

Major international airlines that operate in Vietnam are the national Vietnam Airlines, Korean Air, Singapore Airlines, Thai Airways, China Southern Airlines, Hong Kong Airlines, AirAsia, and Jetstar. Domestic flights are operated and managed by Jetstar, Vietnam Airlines, VASCO, and VietJetAir. Vietnam Airlines cover the most number of destinations in the country.

For long-haul travel within the country, it is better to use flights as buses and trains can be quite unpredictable and, of course, time-consuming.

b) Traveling by Train in Vietnam

Vietnam's railway system covers 1,600 miles with the main line running to and from Ho Chi Minh City in the south and Hanoi in the north of the country. The main line is called Reunification Express. Right through the journey between Ho Chi Minh City and Hanoi, there are many stops that are popular tourist attractions including Nha Trang, Hue and Danang.

The entire trip between the two cities which are about 707 miles apart can take upwards of 40 hours. From Hanoi, you can also travel to Dong Dang and Haiphong. While there are many classes of travel in Vietnamese trains, for expats, it is better to travel in the highest class you can afford. Vietnamese trains can be quite grim, especially the lower class compartments. The seats will be hard and hygiene could be a far cry from what you are accustomed to.

However, the higher class compartments of overnight trains are equipped with cushioned seat-berths. While the country is working hard to improve the services of its railway system, it is yet to reach this goal.

Another way to travel by train is to use private company-run and managed trains. The compartments and seating arrangements are more luxurious and they are cleaner. There are many companies operating private cars such as Fanxipan, Victoria Hotels and Sapaly Train. While these compartments are clean and more luxurious than the state-run ones, they are still dependent on the railway system operated and managed by the state. Therefore, time of travel will not be faster even if you manage to get tickets on these private-owned carriages.

c) Traveling by Buses in Vietnam

Private-run buses are the best options for expats. These buses are called 'open tour' buses and with an 'open' ticket, you can hop on and hop off at any of the stops between Hanoi and Saigon. Most of these vehicles travel on this route only. However, you can also choose to buy tickets individually instead of the 'open' option. These open-tour buses are air-conditioned and have fixed time schedules that are maintained quite diligently by the operators. National state-run buses, on the other hand, are neither air-conditioned nor is there a fixed schedule for them.

d) Traveling by Boat

Waterways are one of the primary modes of transport if you have to travel from village to village once you have left behind the chaotic urban areas and moved into the serene rural locations. You can also travel between Cambodia and Vietnam by boat. At Vietnam, the boats dock and ply from Halong Bay where there are boats to take you on trips to the myriad of islands including the fabulous karst island formations.

e) **Traveling by Car**

Sai Gon traffic at night

Tourists are generally not allowed to drive themselves. Moreover, if you live in Vietnam, driving around can be quite a hassle considering the chaotic traffic conditions and the lack of knowledge of the local areas and roads. It would be better to hire a car and take a driver along for all your trips.

f) Traveling by Scooters, Motorbikes, and Motorcycles

You can also rent a two-wheeler like a scooter or motorbike and travel around in many large cities of Vietnam. You can also get on a motorcycle taxi with a rider who can take you around.

Busy street in Sai Gon, Vietnam

g) Traveling within Cities of Vietnam

Vietnamese Cyclo

Within each city, there are many ways of traveling including the ubiquitous cyclos or the bicycle rickshaws. In some extremely congested cities, cyclos are banned though. You will have to learn great bargaining skills before you choose to use a cyclo for your local travel as they will otherwise charge you exorbitant sums. Motorbike taxis are also available. Prices for both cyclos and motorbike taxis are negotiated and fixed before taking off. You can also find car taxis in all major cities of Vietnam.

Visa Procedures

It is very easy to get a Vietnamese visa. You can complete the application and make the payment online and simply get your visa stamped on your passport on arrival to the country. Here are the steps to follow for applying for a Vietnamese Visa.

1. Visit the government website for visa applications - https://vietnamvisa.govt.vn/
2. There is an online application that you can complete. You will need the following information handy:
3. Your full name
4. Passport details
5. Nationality
6. Type of Visa required
7. Date of your arrival at Vietnam
8. The name of the airport where you will land; the international airports which allow foreigners to enter and leave Vietnam are Hai Phong, Hanoi, Ho Chi Minh City, Da Nang, and Nha Trang
9. You can pay the visa fees online
10. An email approval from the Vietnam Immigration Department will be sent to you
11. Keep a hard copy of this approval letter along with two passport photographs in the stipulated format
12. Simply carry the approval letter, your photos, stamping fee amount, and your passport when you travel
13. When you reach the designated airport in Vietnam, show the documents to the Immigration Officer and your passport will be stamped accordingly

Weather in Vietnam

Ha Long Bay, Vietnam

With a tropical monsoon climate, Vietnam primarily has two seasons including the northeast monsoon between October and April and the southwest monsoon between April and September. Monsoons in Vietnam do not necessarily translate to rain owing to the various regional topography and other geographical conditions in each area. In general, the climate during the northeast monsoon is cool but not very wet and the climate during the southwest monsoon is hot and wet.

The best way to understand weather in Vietnam is to divide the country into three parts including North Vietnam, Central

Vietnam, and South Vietnam. The temperatures across the country are more or less constant all the year round except for some regions in the far north such as Hanoi, which can get very cold in the months of December and January. Also, temperatures in the Central Highlands are cooler as compared to the rest of Vietnam.

a) Southern Vietnam

In Southern Vietnam, especially in the Mekong Delta, the southwest monsoons result in hot, humid, and extremely wet climates with June and July being particularly wetter than the rest of the season. During June and July, you can see flooding in Saigon. Phu Quoc, the island in southern Vietnam is prone to really bad weather including rough seas during this time.

b) Northern Vietnam

Thanks to the northeast monsoon, the weather in Northern Vietnam ranges from cool to cold between October and April and warm to hot during the southwest monsoon time between April to November. In some parts of this region such as Halong Bay and Sapa, heavy mists can be experienced reducing visibility considerably. The driest months here are December and January and the wettest months are July and August.

c) Central Vietnam

Climate-wise, Central Vietnam acts like a transitory phase between Northern and Southern Vietnam. The Truong Son Mountains shield the coastline preventing the rains of the southwest monsoons from reaching there. Therefore, the coast sees less rain than the rest of the country between April and September.

During the northeast monsoon season, this scene is reversed and the northern part of Central Vietnam including Da Nang, Hoi An, Hue, and Dong Na receive a lot of rain as they lie in the way of the oncoming monsoons. Moreover, between August and September, this region is also affected by the typhoons of the Western Pacific Ocean and severe storms rage particularly in Hoi An. The southern part of Central Vietnam is less affected by rain and more or less sees long, sunny summers.

Chapter 6: Cities of Vietnam

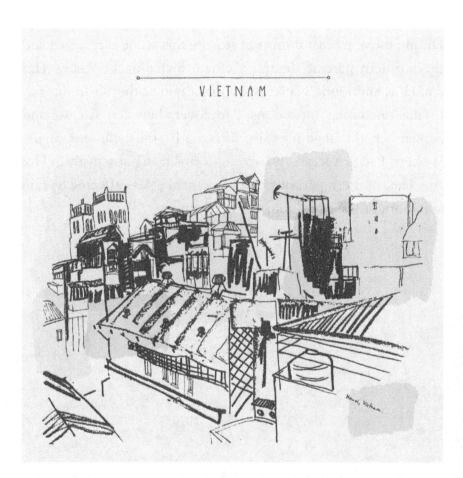

Expats planning to move to Vietnam will not be disappointed with what the country offers. Low cost of living, a vibrant culture and friendly people, all beckon more and more foreigners to settle in this wonderful country. This chapter is dedicated to the different cities in Vietnam that are highly suitable for expat settlement.

It is important that you get all your documentation and paperwork in order before you move to Vietnam. Legally, as an expat, you cannot work in the country without a work permit. Yes, the slow bureaucracy might take time to catch up during which time you might get away with working with no permit. However, the regulatory authorities conduct random checks and if you and/or your employer is caught without the correct paperwork, you will be in jeopardy.

You can come in with a 3-month tourist visa and hunt for a job during that time. When the tourist visa expires, you might have to leave the country before you re-enter. However, that is not a problem because you can take a bus to neighboring Cambodia and come back again; all within the framework of law.

Once you have the paperwork in place, make sure you find a city that matches your lifestyle. Let us look at some of the cities in Vietnam that are great for expat living and you can choose one that is aligned with your needs.

Ho Chi Minh City (Sai Gon)

Ho Chi Minh City (Sai Gon), Vietnam

Known as the hot (stinking) mega city and also as the city that rarely sleeps, more than half the expatriates of Vietnam live in Ho Chi Minh City. With a complex history going back over two millennia, Ho Chi Minh City today is as urban as it can be; green spaces and trees are almost non-existent while traffic and crowds are in excess. While this may sound chaotic to some of you, if you were to speak to the expats living there, they will say that the noise, dynamism, chaos, and crowds are the reasons for them to love the city that is full of excitement and adventure.

With accommodation options to match all kinds of budgets and a multitude of eating places to choose from, Ho Chi Minh City throbs with life. The expat community here is diverse and large and consists of citizens from different parts of the world. Therefore, it is very easy to make friends for new expats here. Although a large number of foreigners settled here are in the teaching profession, since the city is a hub for tourism, manufacturing and information technology, there are plenty of job opportunities available in different professions and domains.

The one thing to be wary of while looking for a job in Ho Chi Minh City is that the locals (who are slowly gaining ground with regards to new-world skills and knowledge) are willing to do the same work at a much lower pay.

Other than great job opportunities, Ho Chi Minh City has plenty of history and culture to soak up. Here are a few interesting places:

1. Cu Chi Tunnels

Underground Cu Chi Tunnel

This infamous yet intricate and huge network of tunnels was used in the even more infamous Vietnam War. The Vietnamese used them to keep entire villages from marauding US troops. These same tunnels also helped the guerilla soldiers take American soldiers by surprise. You can see the ingenious traps set by the Vietnamese to maim and kill US soldiers.

2. War Remnants Museum

War Remnants Museum

Ho Chi Minh City was the center of the Vietnam War and, therefore, natural to be left with war relics and remnants hopefully serving as bad memories no one wants to repeat. The visit to this museum can be a very sobering experience. It contains artifacts from the Vietnam War and the first Indochina War fought against the French.

3. Notre Dame Cathedral

Notre Dame Cathedral, Sai Gon

A brilliant piece of French architecture, the Notre Dame Cathedral in Ho Chi Minh City should not be missed. The cathedral here was built with an intention to recreate the original that is in Paris. Replete with gigantic bell towers and made with French bricks, this cathedral is magnificent and a must-see.

Hanoi

Ha Noi, Capital of Vietnam

With a less cosmopolitan outlook than Ho Chi Minh City, Hanoi is preferred by many expats for its unique feel and rich culture that also goes back many centuries. Another attractive feature of Hanoi is its cooler temperature compared to other parts of the country. There are fewer industries and business establishments in Hanoi because it is the bureaucratic center and the seat of the Communist government. Again, teaching is a common profession among expats living and working in Hanoi.

The street food and coffee will definitely live up to your Vietnamese expectations. Here are a few places of interest in Hanoi:

1. The Old Quarter

Old Quarter, Ha Noi

Located close to Hoan Kiem Lake, the Old Quarter in Hanoi is full of old Buddhist pagodas and temples, colonial buildings, and is also the city's major commercial area. There are streets dedicated to each specific commodity. For example, there are streets where only cotton merchants set up shop. Similarly, there is a jewelry street, herb street, silk street and so forth. Today, many shops of these streets have contemporary items and commodities on sale. Yet, you can get the feel of the original shops and culture left behind by hundreds of years of the old Vietnamese culture.

2. Hoan Kiem Lake

Hoan Kiem Lake (Ho Guom), Ha Noi

Also called Ho Guom Lake, it is one of the most important scenic spots of the city. Hoan Kiem Lake translates to the Lake of the Returned Sword. The lake surrounds the Ngoc Son Temple, built in the 18th century, and is located right in the middle of a small island called Jade Island, which can be accessed via the Rising Sun Bridge or the Huc Bridge. This temple is dedicated to Tran Hung Dao, a brave general of the 13th century who fought against the Yuan Dynasty of China. The temple and the surrounding lake are, perhaps, the most visited places in Hanoi.

3. Thang Long Water Puppet Theater

Traditional Vietnamese water puppet show, Hanoi

With origins dating back to nearly 1000 years ago, water puppetry is unique to Vietnam, in general, and Hanoi, in particular. The highly entertaining show consists of puppets manipulated by puppeteers in a wading pool or a shallow pond.

Da Nang

Dragon River Bridge (Rong Bridge), Da Nang

A booming city that many expats prefer over Ho Chi Minh City and Hanoi, Da Nang is the perfect place for you if you want a beach in your life while living in Vietnam. With amazing beaches on one side and mountainous jungles on the other side, this city is great to explore unknown and remote regions of Vietnam. Here are some places of interest in Da Nang:

1. My Khe Beach

My Khe Beach, Da Nang

With 20 miles of white sand, this beach was named by American soldiers during the Vietnam War. It is believed to be one of the most beautiful beaches in Vietnam. My Khe Beach is great for snorkeling, fishing, jet-skiing, or simply lying on the smooth sand and sunbathing.

2. Marble Mountains

Marble Mountains, Da Nang

Consisting of five marble and limestone hills, the Marble Mountains are located in Hoa Hai District, 9 km south of Da Nang. The five peaks take the names of five elements of nature and are called:

- Thuy Son (water)
- Moc Son (wood)
- Hoa Son (Fire)
- Kim Son (Metal)
- Tho Son (earth)

There are pagoda and Buddhist sanctuaries across the mountains. The locals come here to pray and get their fortune told. Climbing up the steps of the Marble Mountains, you can have some spectacular views that cover My Khe and Non Nuoc beaches

The ancient sculpture of standing Buddha, Marble mountains

3. Son Tra Mountains

Referred to as the Monkey Mountains, it is a national park which is home to rare species of monkeys including the red-faced ones. You can climb up the mountains through the winding roads either on motorcycles or hiking. The Linh Ung Pagoda atop the Son Tra Mountains is a statue of the Goddess of Mercy.

The statue of the Goddess of Mercy in Linh Ung Pagodo, Da Nang

Nha Trang

Since this place is a very popular destination for Russian tourists, tourism is the most thriving industry here and jobs for expats are in this sector only. With a relaxed vibe, a nice quiet beach, Nha Trang is a beautiful place to live in. Many digital nomads are moving in here. Some places of interest in Nha Trang:

1. Po Nagar Cham Towers

These towers date back to between 8th and the 11th century. Built on the peak of Mount Cu Lau, the views from there cover the Cai River. Originally, there were ten buildings each dedicated to different Hindu deities. However, most of the original buildings have been destroyed and today, there are four towers dedicated to the gods of the Cham people.

Cham Towers in Nha Trang

2. Long Son Pagoda

Built in the 19th century, the Long Son Pagoda boasts of some amazing designs of dragon on mosaic tiles. At the peak of the hill (which you can reach by climbing the 150 steps) is a huge white statue of the Buddha sitting on a lotus blossom.

The statue of Buddha sitting on lotus blossom, Long Son

3. Nha Trang Cathedral

Built in French Gothic style and serving the local Catholic community, the Nha Trang Cathedral is considered to be the biggest church in the city. Stunning stained glass windows, a square-shaped clock tower, and a big crucifix are characteristic features of this cathedral. It overlooks the railway station of Nha Trang.

King Cathedral (Stone Church), Nha trang

4. National Oceanographic Museum

Set up in 1922, there are some excellent exhibits of marine life here including more than 20,000 preserved and live marine specimens. The museum which is part of the National Oceanographic Institute of Vietnam offers community and research projects like preservation, breeding programs, coral reefs regeneration, and more.

Vung Tau

Its proximity to Ho Chi Minh City and its laidback lifestyle attracts a lot of expats to Vung Tau. It is only a two-hour bus drive from Vung Tau and Ho Chi Minh City. This quiet beach town is a great place for a home if your job does not require your physical presence every day. Vung Tau is gaining ground as the largest crude oil extraction region in Vietnam because of which the infrastructure here is better than in most other cities of the country. Places of interest in Vung Tau include:

1. Ho Tram Beach

With over 10 km of unspoiled water and beach, the Ho Tram beach is perfect for relaxation and peace. Palm trees and fine sand enhance the beauty of the place. You also have affordable camping facilities and you can eat in any of the numerous seafood stalls set up there. There are many fishing villages and fruit plantations close by that you can visit too.

2. Binh Chau Hot Springs

Locals go to Binh Chau Hot Springs for foot and mud baths. The hot springs are at about 37-degrees Celsius which is just perfect for you. However, in some parts of the hot spring, the water temperature is so high that you can even boil an egg or potatoes!

3. Niet Ban Tinh Xa

The Reclining Buddha statue, Vung Tau

Also known as the Pagoda of the Reclining Buddha or the Temple of Nirvana, Niet Ban Tinh Xa was constructed in 1969. The architectural workmanship and great detailing are amazing to see. The temple also houses a 12-m marble statue of Lord Buddha.

No matter which city you choose to live in, the Vietnamese culture and history are impossible to miss. Whether it is the chaotic Ho Chi Minh City or the quiet laid back Vung Tau town, the thread of Vietnamese culture, history, and legends run right through all the cities of the country.

Chapter 7: Jobs, Cost of Living and Other Critical Details in Vietnam

As Vietnam's economy is moving in the upward direction, more and more job opportunities are available for expats in the country. With nearly 100,000 foreign workers in Vietnam as of 2017, the expat community in the country is growing by leaps and bounds. In the larger cities like Da Nang and Ho Chi Minh City, there are areas that are dedicated places for expats and only foreigners live in these districts. For example, you will find many expats living, socializing, and doing business in:

- **Ho** Chi Minh City's Bui Vien Street
- Hanoi's Luong Ngoc Quyen, Ta Hien, and Dinh Liet districts
- Hoi An Ancient close to Da Nang

Vietnam is slowly opening its cultural and economic doors to foreigners. Therefore, there is a lot of demand for different skills associated with expats, which are reflective of an attempt to bridge the gap between Vietnam and the rest of the world.

Job Opportunities in Vietnam

1. Foreign Language Teachers

Education has always been revered and respected in the Vietnamese culture. The poor Vietnamese look to education as a means of escape from poverty. The middle class looks at education with an intention to climb the social ladder even further. For the richer and the upper-middle class section, education is a tool that they believe empowers them to manage and enhance their family's success and money.

With the opening of Vietnam's doors to multinational businesses from across the globe, a lot more foreign companies are doing business here and creating job opportunities for the local Vietnamese. This has also an increased the demand for knowledge of English and many other foreign languages among the locals to enhance their chances of landing jobs at these big conglomerates.

A lot of foreign language institutes are coming up all over Vietnam to meet this increasing demand. These institutes hire foreigners as language teachers thereby giving expats great job opportunities in this sector. The pay is good too and based on the experience and qualifications; an expat can earn anywhere between $15 and $100 per hour of teaching.

In fact, there are foreign language centers that are opened, managed, and run by foreigners. Long-term tourists and backpackers teach English, French, Spanish, Japanese, Chinese, etc to earn extra income. Of course, with increasing knowledge among the local Vietnamese, expats need to hone their language skills and be prepared to meet the high demands of the students in order to get and maintain lucrative teaching positions.

2. Real Estate Managers

The real estate market in Vietnam is witnessing unprecedented growth with some pockets quoting land prices that are higher than even those quoted in Tokyo and more advanced cities. This boom in the market is primarily driven by foreign investments pouring into Vietnam. Moreover, the state is also funding infrastructure and other city-improvement projects, which are driving real estate prices up.

For example, on the island of Phu Quoc, the provincial government invested a lot of money to build luxury hotels, resorts, and other project resulting in land prices becoming 10 times greater in a very short period. Additionally, several large global conglomerates are investing in the property market of Vietnam acquiring strategic projects and land areas from the state.

New laws have been passed in the country by virtue of which foreigners can buy (as a long-term lease) property with the lease period of up to 50 years and with a renewable clause too. These consumer-friendly laws combined with a lot of speculation and hoarding has resulted in the mushrooming of multiple real estate companies and real estate developers.

As an expat, with the right knowledge and the right connections, it is possible to be a successful real estate broker brokering big deals resulting in large commissions.

3. Tour Operators

A lot of foreign tourists are making a beeline to Vietnam thanks to its affordability wonderfully complemented by its rich cultural heritage. Many of the local tour operators are unable to understand what exactly foreigners expect from their Vietnam traveling experiences because of their own lack of experience in the outside world.

However, expats living in Vietnam are perfect for this. They are well-versed with foreign cultures as well as local Vietnamese cultures. With this powerful combination, expat tour operators are able to offer traveling and touring options that synchronize expectations with the local availability to foreign tourists. Many expats are earning good income as tour operators for foreign tourists.

4. Restaurateurs and Boarding House Management

The food and accommodation sector in Vietnam is a highly lucrative one for expats as foreigners are permitted to set up boarding and lodging facilities here. There are a lot of foreign investments in this industry as well with global brands like McDonald's, Starbucks, KFC, and many more setting up shop in Vietnam.

Moreover, expats and foreigners are setting up their own family-owned and family-run food and lodging businesses in multiple cities across the country and thanks to their excellent hospitality, they have managed to garner many loyal and repeat customers. The locals too love to walk into these establishments. Integrating the unique cultures and cuisine from their own country with local flavor, many expats have managed to start, hold, and expand their food and lodging businesses in Vietnam.

5. Investment Consultants

With increasing foreign direct investments pouring in, Vietnam is a hub for investment consultants with the right combination of local knowledge and overseas expectations. Yes, setting up new businesses in Vietnam is highly lucrative for foreigners. Yet, there is a lot of red-tape, bureaucratic procedures, and other legal hassles that deter foreigners from setting up new businesses here.

Investors need trained and knowledgeable people who can guide them through the various processes including finding the right location, signing rental/lease agreements and contracts with the landlord, complete application documentation, etc. Once the registration process is completed successfully, other elements of the business including getting approvals and sanctions from the concerned government department, opening bank accounts, etc need to be done as well. Government policies in Vietnam are not very clear-cut and can be interpreted in various ways requiring multiple meetings and consultations with state-controlled regulatory authorities.

Considering these problems, nearly all foreign business investors seek local professional help right from the beginning. An expat living Vietnam with great business skills and knowledge about local requirements is the perfect fit for such a profession. Therefore, you will find a lot of expats in this segment helping people from their own countries or from other foreign countries to establish and expand new businesses in Vietnam.

The charges are usually taken in the form of a commission, which depends on the size and the complexities involved in setting the business, and yes, it can be very lucrative. Therefore, expats well-versed with the local legal, administrative, and business requirements can take up investment consultancy as a great career.

6. Content Creator and Other Online Options

As per one of the latest statistics, nearly 67% of the Vietnamese population has access to the Internet. By the way, Internet costs in Vietnam are very economical. As more and more people from all over the world are reaching out to the Internet to hire freelancers in various industries, people living in Vietnam are also privy to this segment.

As expats living here, it is quite easy for you to set up your own freelancing agency and work from home by creating content or doing any other kind of online work through the internet. The local people are still catching up on the skills needed for this domain leaving the market open for expats whose language and other knowledge levels are much higher than that of many local people.

Many expats living in Vietnam work as full-time content creators creating website designs, writing, doing video-blogs, and other online marketing works. They work with both local organizations including book publishers and foreign companies from different segments as geographical distances are hardly any kind of deterrent for online workers.

Summarily, expats living in Vietnam have plenty of job opportunities with foreigners as well as the local people and business entities. Owing to a better skill set both in terms of domain expertise and communication skills, the remuneration packages of expats are generally better than those of locals. In fact, many expats juggle different jobs simultaneously making more money than they would have made in their own country.

Cost of Living and Quality of Life

Here is a small breakup regarding the cost of living in Vietnam for expats. This lifestyle with these costs are associated with middle class and yet will get you all of life's necessities required to live a happy and fulfilling life in this amazing and wondrous country. The currency of Vietnam is Vietnamese Dong and the exchange rate with US$ is approximately: US$ 1 = 22000 Vietnamese Dong (approximation only). Total costs per month range between $700 and $1500 depending on your lifestyle. This amount (for a single person) includes rent, food, Internet, and other expenses. Housing costs have already been spoken about in chapters.

Low cost of living and availability of cheap food and accommodation is a sure shot combination to draw tourists, travelers, backpackers, and even new settlers to Vietnam. The low cost of living is connected to very low pay earned by the locals. The monthly income for a local person ranges from $150 to about $500 (for the really higher earners). Young expat entrepreneurs and new-age technologists prefer to set up home in Ho Chi Minh City while the older generation and the retirees prefer to live in Hoi An and Hanoi. Let us look at a few cities in specific with regards to cost of living and quality of life.

a) Hanoi

One of the most ancient districts of Vietnam and is home to multiple museums, old colonial buildings and ancient pagodas, Hanoi is situated on the banks of the Red River. With a vibrant nightlife, Hanoi is multicultural in outlook combining influences from Russia, China, and France.

Most expats in Hanoi are ESL (English as a Second Language) teachers. The cost of living for such people ranges between $600 and $900 in Hanoi. The maximum expenditure would be towards rent and if you choose an accommodation with modern amenities including gym, swimming pool, 24-hour security, then the cost of living could go up.

b) Ho Chi Minh City

Also known as Saigon, Ho Chi Minh City is home to young expat entrepreneurs and the digital nomads. With access to cheap high-speed internet, getting online is the easiest way to make money in this city. The cost of living in Saigon ranges between $750 and $1300.

With access to amazing street foods that you can eat three times a day seven days a week, this place is perfect for the young and yuppie. Ho Chi Minh City played a very important role in the Vietnam War, and the attractions here are a heady combination of the old and the new. Relics from the War and well-maintained colonial buildings will leave you feeling sad for the mindless loss of lives and happy for the grit and determination of the Vietnamese people to not just survive but also thrive.

c) Hoi An

With a lower cost of living than the above two cities, you can live a happy life with amounts ranging from $550 to $800 in Hoi An. With this cost, you will have access to a fairly large two-bedroom accommodation. With canals running through the city, Hoi An is home to multiple historical places including French colonial buildings, Chinese shop houses, and ancient temples. This delightful town draws many visitors from all over the world.

Bridge at night in Hoi An

Chapter 8: The Best of Vietnam and the Worst of Vietnam

Every country has something good and bad to offer visitors and settlers and locals as well and Vietnam is no exception. There are good and bad things in this country and knowing about both will give you a balanced view of Vietnam. Moreover, when you are aware of potential problems, then you can work out solutions beforehand and be prepared to counter them.

Worst Things about Vietnam

1. Overcharged

Another common problem in other countries too, being overcharged is rampant in Vietnam. In fact, even locals end up paying more for products and services. Here are some tips to avoid being overcharged:

- Always choose a restaurant that has prices clearly quoted in the menu.
- Clearly, ask for the price of any product or service you choose to buy. Know and agree on the price beforehand
- Look around, do some research and find out prices from everywhere else and then make your choice. In Vietnam, there is no need to hurry. So take your time to be careful.

As a traveler, this might be a problem for you. However, if you choose to make Vietnam your home, you will learn the ways and means to ensure you pay the right amount for everything.

2. *Taxi Problems*

Yes, this could come under the 'overcharged' heading. Yet, it requires special attention and, therefore, I have put it separately. Taxis can scam you in more ways than one and both locals and foreigners are victims

- They could tamper with their meters resulting in charges going at double rates
- They could drive you in circles to increase the charge

- Here are some tips to avoid being scammed by taxis:
- Use Google Maps to find the correct distance to where you want to go. Simply multiply the per-kilometer charge into the distance
- Make sure the price is fixed before you get into the taxi
- Choose established and reputable taxi companies. You can also use Uber and Grab for your trips.

3. *Hygiene*

Street foods are amazing in Vietnam and you will find it very difficult to resist it. However, food hygiene is a big problem in this country. Most of the time, street foods are unclean and unhealthy. In addition to the vendors not preparing them well, the hot and humid climates could play havoc with the quality of ingredients and prepared foods.

In fact, if you want to completely avoid problems from the effects of unhygienic food, then you must stay away from street food entirely. The government is still working on trying to implement laws with regard to hygiene in the country. However, if you find it impossible to stay away from outside food completely, then make sure to take the following precautions:

- Go only to established and reputed restaurants. Make sure the place is clean before you order your food
- Carry medication with you always

Another tip is to ensure you are eating piping hot food. Check under the soup or any pot and ensure that the stove is on and the food is bubbling gently. Hot food reduces risks of upset stomach.

4. Traffics

Traffic accidents are common in Vietnam. While the reasons could be many including rash driving, ignorant pedestrians, and more, it makes sense to be very careful while you are on the road. Here are some tips to avoid being embroiled in a traffic accident:

- Public transportation may not be fast and clean. But they are very safe. You are safely ensconced in a big box and little motorbikes scurrying around will do you no harm
- Taxis are the next bet for safety. If you cannot afford taxis, then use the bus
- Walking is another great way of avoiding accidents. You are in control of your movements and you can take precautions multiple times before crossing the road, etc.

5. Customer Service

While people are friendly and nice, you cannot really expect impeccable service from everyone. The primary reason is lack of knowledge of English and other foreign languages. Moreover, efficiency is still in its infancy in the world of economics in Vietnam. So, we need to be patient as the country attempts to reach world standards when it comes to service and efficiency. Here are some tips to draw out good service from the locals:

119

- Learn some basic amount of Vietnamese language and combine it with effective body language to avoid miscommunications and misunderstandings.
- Make friends with locals and they will help you with great places to eat, visit, and enjoy

The Best Things in Vietnam

1. Amazing Cultural Melting Pot

Starting from China way back in the second century B.C., Vietnam has been attacked time and again by other nations including colorization by the French, the Portuguese, and attacks from Japan. The good thing that came about from these invasions is that Vietnam is now an amazing cultural and historical melting pot with influences from China, Europe, Japan, Russia, and more.

Even though the government is atheistic, there are different religions that are practiced and tolerated admirably by the people of Vietnam. Christianity, a late entrant into the country, co-mingles peacefully with ancient Taoism, Buddhism, and Confucianism. The annual festivals, like tet, are harbingers of peace, harmony, and joy both for the locals and the expats. Colonial buildings and ancient temples share space like they were made for each, other and the integration of the new with the old is seamless.

2. Landscape

The landscape in Vietnam has to be seen to be believed. The ones at Halong Bay, the Sapa Terraces in the north, and at the iconic Mekong Delta stand out. Halong Bay is a UNESCO World Heritage site is home to numerous limestone islands. As you cruise on the water through these islands, the landscapes you will be treated to are amazing.

Vietnam is also home to some of the biggest caves in the world. Replete with magnificently formed stalactites and stalagmites, these caves can be explored from underwater as well. The spectacular waterfalls in the Central Highlands, wonderful range of flora and fauna in the vast forest regions there are places for capturing some great pictures.

The Sapa Terraces (that usually grow paddy) when flooded with water shimmer beautifully until the rice shoots push through the water layer. These green shoots became darker slowly and, then turn to a beautiful golden yellow by the time they are ready to harvest. Each sight is a sight to behold.

The Mekong Delta in Southern Vietnam is a river that is flowing down from the Tibetan Highlands. This river widens at the Mekong Delta before joining the South China Sea. The Mekong Delta is a very fertile region producing agricultural products both for domestic consumption and for exports.

3. The People of Vietnam

Tourism has had a huge impact on the economy of Vietnam and yes, a few unscrupulous agents and companies are out to make a quick dishonest buck during the boom. However, the people not directly connected to the tourism industry such as the farmers and the fisher folk are very hospitable and a pleasure to interact with.

If you are only traveling for a short time in Vietnam, you could choose to stay for a while in a home-stay in one of the Vietnamese villages where you can directly experience and live the life these simple folks lead. Many of the houses in the villages are built on stilts for protection from flooding effects common during the monsoons.

The Northern Highlands is home to multiple ethnic tribes that are working hard to keep their culture and history alive amidst the encroaching modernity. They still wear ethnic clothes, sing and dance the way their ancestors did, and live off nature without being greedy. The crafts made and sold by these ethnic tribes can be great Vietnamese souvenirs.

4. The Cuisine

Asian cuisine is catching the fancy of the world, thanks to the leaders, India and China. However, Vietnamese cuisine is slowly but surely finding its own niche in the world cuisine market. While there are excellent restaurants all over the country, the best way to get the authentic taste of Vietnam is to walk the streets and indulge in the street foods.

With rice as the staple ably supported by an amazing range of seafood, soups, and fresh fruits and vegetables, Vietnamese is slowly coming out of its cocoon and ready to spread its butterfly wings.

5. Cost of Living

Undoubtedly one of the cheapest countries to live in, Vietnam can offer a lot with little money. The public transport is inexpensive and although the infrastructure has a long way to reach world standards, it is moving in the right direction.

6. *Gender Equality in Vietnam*

The Vietnamese women are a strong lot and this strong attitude goes back many years when women held the purse strings in her family. The wife has always been the treasurer and the keeper of money and gold in any family. The children and the husband are also expected to help the lady in the kitchen and in doing other domestic chores.

Women were allowed to run their businesses and could manage and operate any financial endeavor undertaken by the family. These businesses could be in the form of a little grocery store or a coffee shop or anything else. The only jobs that are not usually done by women include going out to the sea for fishing and being a taxi operator. All other jobs are done with fervor by the women of Vietnam. They are a hardy lot and Western women have a lot to learn from them.

Almost all the stalls in the market are run by women. In fact, one of the richest private capitalists in Vietnam is a lady. The women are stall owners and they are the shoppers as well. Confucianism gives the provider to the male in the family. However, Vietnamese women bring up their daughters by teaching them (most times, by being an example themselves) that everyone needs to have financial independence.

Most women make themselves financially independent by investing in gold and gems. Women have an elaborate system of boxes, purses, jars, and other furtive containers in which they hide the money saved during the month. The best thing about these hiding places is that it is hardly ever opened in front of and seen by the men in the family! While for an outsider, the desire for gold jewelry might come across as mere vanity, in truth, this is the women's way of creating a stable financial set up for herself.

The worst things in Vietnam are not necessarily a dampener. They are simply obstacles that naturally come in the way of an underdeveloped nation as it struggles to keep up with the development of the rest of the world. With a bit of care and patience, your Vietnamese experience will not only be wonderful but also a great eye-opener as you come to terms with the various cultural differences that exist even as you interact and meet more and more friendly Vietnamese right through your journey.

Conclusion

I would like to end this book with the inevitable debate over which is the better city; Hanoi or Ho Chi Minh City. Well, there are no right/wrong answers for this. I would like to say that Hanoi represents traditional and the old aspects of Vietnam while Ho Chi Minh City represents the chic and modern aspects of Vietnam. And both are beautiful in their own rights.

Vietnam is a fairly large country covering a long range of latitudes resulting in distinct climatic differences, which, in turn, lead to certain local customs that are unique to each region in the country. Yes, there are negatives in this wonderful place. But, every time you want to criticize it, remember the long, difficult, and violent struggles for freedom from immemorial.

The people of Vietnam are still recovering from one of the worst wars of the 20th century, and it is but natural that we cut them some slack. That is what compassion is all about. Instead of finding faults with the systems there, it makes more sense to take extra precautions to ensure you are not robbed or cheated.

Moreover, the great food, the great landscapes, the great monuments, the wonderful people, and the rich cultural heritage more than makes up for the negatives of this very beautiful country. If you are planning to visit Vietnam to first test the waters before deciding to settle down, then it is important to go with an open mind and learn and accept the customs and rituals even if they seem weird and different to you. After all, diversity is what makes our planet so colorful and opulent.

It is, indeed, ironic that the very country the US warred against is now one of the most popular destinations for traveling Americans. This only talks about the stunning beauty and the kind and gentle hospitality of the Vietnamese. Go and make it a part of your life. Yes, there are going to be adjustment issues but none that are not surmountable. Moreover, on the other side of the adjustment challenges lies a contented, peaceful, and happy life in one of the most beautiful and amazing countries of the world.

Bonus

As a way of saying thanks for your purchase, we're offering a special gift that's exclusive to my readers.

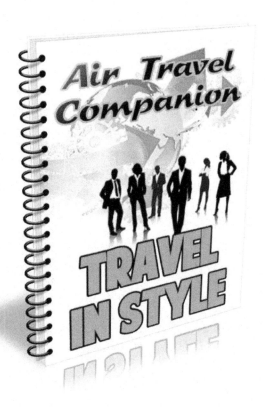

Visit this link below to claim your bonus.

http://dingopublishing.com/bonus/

More books from us

Bushido: The Samurai Code of Honour

Link: http://dingopublishing.com/book/bushido/

The Samurai were highly-skilled warriors, fighting for various reasons, even establishing the feudal era known as Edo, with a social caste system that put them on the top. The Samurai ruled Japan for several years, fought wars for 700, and eventually became obsolete.

But, their traditions and codes are not gone from history. They live on today. Everyone can learn a little something from the Samurai, including how to live a better life. Honoring people, staying loyal, and defending others when it is right are all virtues of the Samurai that can be continued today.

You are going to learn of the eight virtues, the history of the Samurai, some of the most famous warriors, and then you will discover how you can apply their lifestyle to the modern world. Wouldn't it be nice if people returned to a more chivalrous nature, where lying and devious acts are not acceptable? Where being honest, sincere, and courageous are looked upon with reverence?

The Code of the Samurai or Bushido as written by Inazo Nitobe can teach us a lot about living a decent and kind life. Discover how you can uphold the traditions of highly-skilled warriors, even if you are just a regular person.

Japanese Etiquette

http://dingopublishing.com/book/japanese-etiquette/

The Japanese people have an extensive range of customs, rituals, and forms of etiquette for all aspects of their lives. These forms of etiquette are not only interesting for non-Japanese but also open our eyes to the fact that despite the huge strides Japan has made in terms of modern-day advancement in technologies, the age-old customs and traditions are still a deeply-embedded part of their society.

They revere and respect their customs, traditions, and other forms of etiquette and expect people visiting from other countries to do so too. Similarly, the Japanese people are equally respectful of other people's traditions, customs, and etiquette and work hard to understand them so that they don't make a mistake when they visit other countries.

Taking a page out of their etiquette book, it makes a lot of sense to learn about the Japanese forms of etiquette so that we can be prepared to do the right thing at the right time in the right place when we travel to Japan. Moreover, knowing about the culture of another country is a fabulous way of opening our minds and celebrating world differences.

With the etiquette tips in this book, you will be able to handle the expectations of the courteous and polite people of Japan in terms of good behaviour and manners. Most of the people are happy to welcome guests and tourists with open arms and will be even more obliged to do their best to make your stay in their country happy and worthwhile if you show an effort to replicate their etiquette norms and requirements.

(Book excerpt is available on next page)

Book Excerpt: Japanese Etiquette

http://dingopublishing.com/book/japanese-etiquette/

Chapter 1: The Use of Names

One of the most important elements of Japanese etiquette is to be aware of how to address people and how to use names in different social and business settings.

Addressing People with Respect

San is a commonly used respectful expression that is put at the end of people's names while addressing them. San can be used when using the first name or the last name of the concerned individual. Also, san is used for all people irrespective of marital status or gender.

Sama is a term that is more appropriate in a formal setting and is to be used after the family name. Also, you must remember that you must use san or sama after everyone else's name (whom you wish to show respect to) but not after your own name. Here are some examples of the use of san and sama:

- Smith-san (Mr. Smith)
- Michael-san (Mr. Michael)
- Sandra-san (Ms. Sandra)

- Smith-sama (Mr. Smith again but to be used in a formal setting only)
- Tanaka-sama (Ms. Tanaka)

Another way of respectful address is by using the job title of the person along with his or her name. This works in a scenario where you need to address your superior at work or your teacher at school. For example, you can say Brown-sensei (Brown teacher; sensei is teacher in Japanese) instead of saying Brown-sama. Or bucho-san which is referring to your department head; bucho is head in Japanese.

In business environments, using surname instead of given or first name is more respectful. Use of one's job title instead of their name is also well accepted in Japanese business circles. This subtlety of using surnames instead of first names might come across as a bit stiff for some non-Japanese. However, you must remember that most Japanese are uncomfortable using first names.

However, there are a few Japanese citizens with a lot of exposure to Western cultures that have come to accept being addressed by their first names. Some of them have taken this even further and have created nicknames for themselves, which they embrace happily. You can use these nicknames too along with san or sama depending on the level of formality of the setting.

The final tip here is to remember that you can never go wrong using the surname with the san or sama suffix. For all else, it would be prudent to ask around and then make a sensible choice of addressing the concerned person. The convenience of san cannot be underestimated considering that it is unisex and, therefore, you don't have to worry about how to address people through email especially if the Japanese names are not clearly gender-specific.

Also, if someone is addressing you with the san suffix, accept it as a compliment. That's the intention of the Japanese name-calling etiquette.

Addressing Family and Friends

In Japan, addressing family members and friends also calls for politeness and respect though there is less formality than the use of san or sama. There is a plain form and there is a polite form when it comes to addressing family and friends. Here are a few examples:

- Otto or goshujin – husband
- Tsuma or okusan - wife
- Okoson – child in a polite form and Kodomo – child in a plain form
- Otosan – father in a polite form and Chichi – father in a plain form
- Okāsan – mother in a polite form and haha – mother in a plain form
- musukosan – son in a polite form and musuko – son in a plain form
- musumesan – daughter in a polite form and musume – daughter in a plain form

- otōtosan – older brother in a polite form and ani – older brother in a plain form
- onēsan – older sister in a polite form and ane – older sister in a plain form
- imōtosa – younger sister in a polite form and imōto – younger sister in a plain form
- tomodachi – friend

During conversations, shujin is used to refer to one's own husband and otto is used to refer to someone else's husband. Tsuma is used to refer to one's own wife and kanai is used to refer to someone else's wife

Here's the trick when it comes to using the plain form or the polite form. If you are addressing an older member of the family, then you must use the polite form. When addressing the younger members of the family (spouse also comes in the category), you can use the plain form. To get this right, you must also know the difference between referring to someone and addressing someone.

Referring to someone means you are not talking to the person but are referring to him or her in a conversation with someone else. Addressing someone, on the other hand, is talking to the person directly.

Commonly Used Japanese Expressions

While we are at this, let me also give you the top five commonly used expressions in Japanese conversations:

Yatta – I did it! – You can use this term whenever you have accomplished or been offered a great job or have won something. All these occasions can be classified under the 'Yatta' category.

Honto – Really? – This expression is used to let the person speaking to you know that you are listening to what is being said.

Â, SÔ DESU KA – I see – Also, a conversational bit of phraseology letting your partner (the one who is talking to you) know you are getting what is being said. A nod invariably accompanies this expression.

Mochiron – of course! – An expression of confidence

Zenzen – not at all – a phrase of emphatic denial (in a polite way) used for situations such as when someone asks you, "Am I disturbing you?" and you politely say, "zenzen."

Chapter 2: Greetings and Body Language Etiquette

There are many ways of greeting people when you meet them. This chapter is dedicated to these Japanese greeting methods.

Bowing

Bowing, or bending at the waist level, is a form of appreciation and respect shown by the person who is bowing to the person who is being bowed to. Bowing is a common form of greeting used along with:

- Good morning - ohayo gozaimasu
- Hello, good afternoon - konnichi wa
- With words of apology or gratitude (arigato)

There are three types of bows depending on how deep the waist is bent. These three types include:

The casual bow (eshaku bow)

Bending at a 15-degree angle, the casual bow also entails a slight tipping of the head. The eshaku bow is used when casual greetings are passed between people or when you pass someone belonging to a higher social status. Casual greetings in the form of good morning or good afternoon or thank you are sufficient by themselves. Yet, when used along with the eshaku bow makes the greeting more heartfelt.

The business bow (keirei bow)

This bow entails bending your torso at 30 degrees and is used when entering and/or leaving a meeting or conference or while greeting customers.

Deep bow (saikeirei bow)

This is the politest form of bowing in Japan and entails lowering the torso by 45 degrees. It is used to express very deep feelings of regret (apology) or gratitude.

Clasping Hands (Gassho)

Bringing both the palms together and clasping them in front of the chest is referred to as gassho. This form of greeting has its origins in Buddhism. Today, it is used before starting a meal and after finishing the meal along with the word, 'itadakimasu.' The word, 'itadakimasu,' means to receive or to accept an item or gift. It expresses gratitude for the food and for the person(s) who prepared the meal.

Bye-Bye

While 'sayonara' is the Japanese word for saying goodbye, the phrase 'bye-bye;' is also commonly used in the country. There is a subtle difference in the way the hand gesture works with sayonara. While in the West, you would open and close your palm as you lift your hand, in Japan, your open palms are waved from left to right and back. The hand is lifted high above your head so that the other person can see it and then the open palms are waved from left to right and back in a broad arch. The eshaku bow is also used commonly while saying bye-bye.

Shaking Hands

Although bowing is the more appropriate Japanese form of greeting, the handshake has come to be an accepted form of greeting, especially in a business setting. However, it is important to note that the handshake of the Japanese is far limper than the 'firm handshake' of the Western culture. This is easy to understand considering that the Japanese culture does not allow for too much physical contact, especially in public.

Body Language Etiquette

Nodding is an important gesture in Japan. When you are talking to someone, it is important that you nod often to imply comprehension. Your nod is telling the speaker that you are listening to him or her, and you are understanding what the person is trying to say.

Silence is an accepted form of nonverbal communication. There is no need to chatter merely to keep a conversation going. Silence is, in fact, an expected means of communication. Talk only when addressed or when it is your turn to do so.

Standing very close to a Japanese person is considered rude and uncomfortable. Avoid touching as much as possible except for that first handshake (the bow is a better option).

Making prolonged eye contact when talking to someone is also considered rude in Japanese culture.

Hugging, shoulder slapping, and other forms of physical contact are also to be avoided, especially in public. The Japanese frown on any outward show of affection of any kind.

Using your forefinger to beckon is disallowed. The Japanese way of beckoning calls for extending your right arm and bending the wrist in the downward direction. You are not allowed to beckon any person older than or senior to you.

How to Sit Correctly

Sitting in Japanese style calls for sitting on the floor and in an upright position. Even meals are had while sitting on the floor with low tables for the food. For tea ceremonies, it is mandatory to sit on the floor.

Both genders use the kneeling, or the seiza, posture to sit in a formal environment. It can get uncomfortable after some time for people (especially Westerners) who are not used to this way of sitting. In modern times, foreigners are exempted from sitting on the floor. In fact, many modern Japanese also find it difficult to sit like this for long. In casual environments, it is common to see men sitting cross-legged and women sitting with both their legs to one side.

If you are sitting on a chair, you are expected to sit with both your feet firmly placed on the ground. You cannot cross your legs or place your ankle on the knee while sitting on the chair.

The seating order works something like this: the most important person (usually the customer or the guest) is furthest away from the door. The place that is farthest away from the door is considered to be the good side in Japanese culture.

If there is a tokonoma (an alcove decorated with a hanging scroll accompanied by a flower arrangement), then the guest is usually placed in front of it. The least important person or the host takes the place closest to the door.

Also, in a business environment, all the people from the same company are seated on the same side of the table. When you visit Japanese businesses, it is common for the receptionist to show you your seat. If you don't see this happening, it might be prudent to ask before taking a seat.

Japanese Etiquette – The Essential Guide to Japanese Traditions, Customs, and Etiqutte

Find out more at:

http://dingopublishing.com/book/japanese-etiquette/

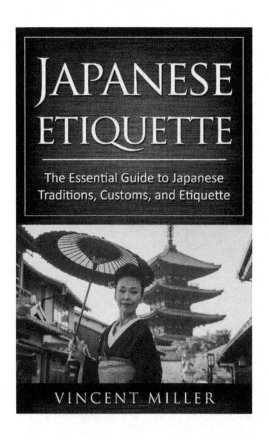

Thanks again for purchasing this book.

We hope you enjoy it

Don't forget to claim your free bonus:

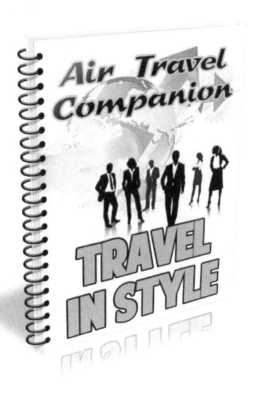

Visit this link below to claim your bonus now:

http://dingopublishing.com/bonus/

Made in the USA
Monee, IL
02 November 2019